FRIENDS
OF ACPL

W9-AFR-189

FAVORITE FOOTBALL TEAMS

NEW YORK GIANTS

BY K. C. KELLEY

THE CHILD'S WORLD®

1980 Lookout Drive • Mankato, MN 56003-1705

800-599-READ • www.childsworld.com

ACKNOWLEDGMENTS

The Child's World®: Mary Berendes, Publishing Director

Shoreline Publishing Group, LLC: James Buckley, Jr.,
 Production Director

The Design Lab: Kathleen Petelinsek, Design;
 Gregory Lindholm, Page Production

PHOTOS

Cover: Focus on Football

Interior: AP/Wide World: 9, 17, 18, 21; Focus on Football: 5, 6, 11, 13, 22, 25,
 27; Stockexpert: 14

Published in the United States of America.

LIBRARY OF CONGRESS
CATALOGING-IN-PUBLICATION DATA

Kelley, K. C.

  New York Giants / by K.C. Kelley.

     p. cm. — (Favorite football teams)

  Includes bibliographical references and index.

  ISBN 978-1-60253-317-2 (library bound : alk. paper)

  1. New York Giants (Football team)—History—Juvenile literature.

I. Title. II. Series.

  GV956.N4K45 2009

  796.332'64097471—dc22   2009009067

COPYRIGHT

Copyright © 2010 by The Child's World®.
All rights reserved. No part of this book may be
reproduced or utilized in any form or by any means
without written permission from the publisher.

TABLE OF CONTENTS

Go, Giants!

In football, being a giant would really help, right? You'd be very hard to tackle. A **touchdown** would be only a few steps away. The ball would be hard to hold in your huge fingers, though! New York has a famous team of giants—the New York Giants football team! Read on to find out about this old and powerful team.

Here come the Giants! Star quarterback Eli Manning runs onto the field before a game.

5

Who Are the New York Giants?

The New York Giants play in the National Football League (NFL). They are one of 32 teams in the NFL. The NFL includes the National Football Conference (NFC) and the American Football Conference (AFC). The Giants play in the East Division of the NFC. The winner of the NFC plays the winner of the AFC in the **Super Bowl**. The Giants have been the NFL champions seven times!

No one gets past the Giants defense! On this play, the men in blue surround a Seattle Seahawks runner.

Where They Came From

The Giants are one of the NFL's oldest teams. They played their first game in 1925. The Mara family has owned the team since then. Tim Mara was the first owner. His son Wellington was in charge until he died in 2005. Today, Wellington's son John runs the team. The Giants have always had the same name. They have always played in the same city. Very few teams can say that!

In 1997, Wellington Mara (left) was elected to the Pro Football Hall of Fame. He was joined by former Giants star Frank Gifford.

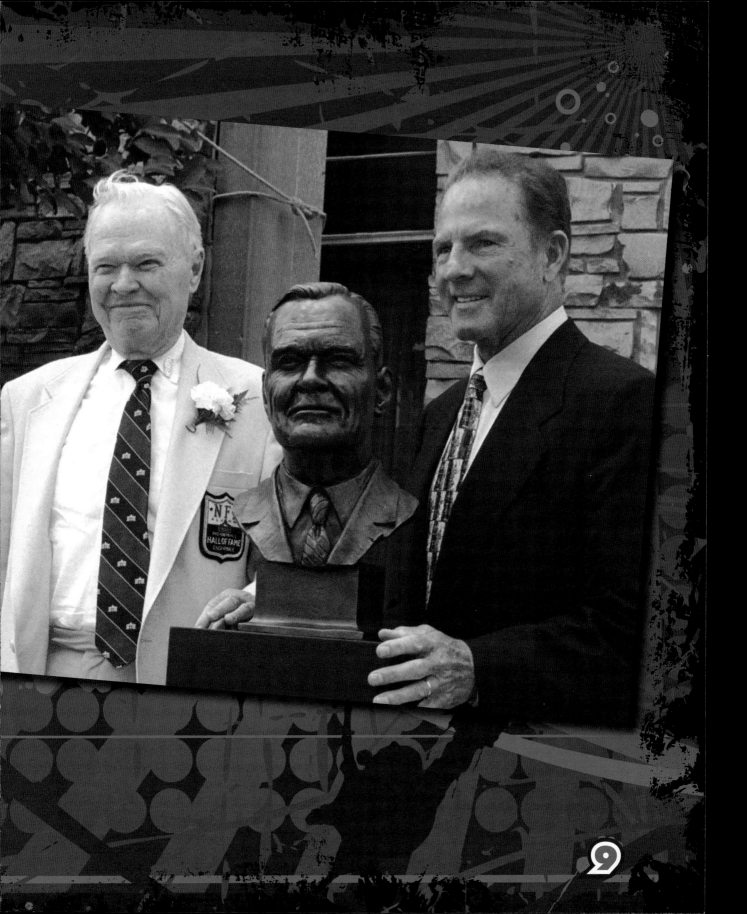

3 1833 05780 8070

Who They Play

The Giants play 16 games each season. There are three other teams in the NFC East. They are the Dallas Cowboys, the Philadelphia Eagles, and the Washington Redskins. Every year, the Giants play each of those teams twice. They also play other teams in the AFC and NFC. The Giants and Cowboys have a fierce **rivalry**. Their games are always tough battles!

The Giants and Cowboys have had many head-to-head battles over the years. Here, they face off at the line of scrimmage.

11

Where They Play

The New York Giants actually play in New Jersey! Giants Stadium is in East Rutherford, New Jersey. The stadium opened in 1976. Fans in the parking lots can see the tall buildings of New York City in the distance. The Giants share their stadium with the New York Jets, another NFL team. They take turns playing home games there. Before they played in New Jersey, the Giants played in Yankee Stadium. In 2010, they are supposed to move into a new Giants Stadium!

At Giants Stadium, fans often have a cookout in the parking lot before the game. It's called "tailgating."

13

goalpost

end zone

red zone

sideline

midfield

hash mark

red zone

goalpost

end zone

FOOTBALL

10 20 30 40 50 40 30 20 10

10 20 30 40 50 40 30 20 10

The Football Field

An NFL field is 100 yards long. At each end is an **end zone** that is another 10 yards deep. Short white **hash marks** on the field mark off every yard. Longer lines mark every five yards. Numbers on the field help fans know where the players are. Goalposts stand at the back of each end zone. On some plays, a team can kick the football through the goalposts to earn points. During the game, each team stands along one sideline of the field. The field at Giants Stadium is covered with **artificial**, or fake, grass. Most outdoor stadiums have real grass.

During a game, the two teams stand on the sidelines. They usually stand near midfield, waiting for their turns to play. Coaches walk on the sidelines, too, along with cheerleaders and photographers.

Big Days!

The New York Giants have had many great moments in their long history. Here are three of the greatest:

1934: On a frozen field, the Giants trailed in the NFL Championship Game. They put on sneakers to play the second half. They didn't slip anymore, and they won the game!

1987: The Giants won their first Super Bowl. They beat the Denver Broncos, 39–20. They won another Super Bowl four years later.

2008: What a game! The Giants won another Super Bowl by scoring in the final minute. Eli Manning threw a touchdown pass with just a few seconds left. The Giants beat the New England Patriots, 17–14. It was the Patriots' first loss of the whole season!

What a catch! The Giants' David Tyree (85) caught this long pass to set up a game-winning touchdown as the Giants beat the Patriots.

Tough Days!

The Giants can't win all their games. Some games or seasons don't turn out well. The players keep trying to play their best, though! Here are some painful memories from the Giants' history:

1973-1974: The Giants had two of their worst seasons—back to back! They won only four of the 28 games they played.

2001: The Giants were happy to make the Super Bowl. But the Baltimore Ravens kept the Giants' **offense** from scoring. Baltimore won, 34-7.

2003: The Giants led the San Francisco 49ers 38-14 in a playoff game. But the 49ers came back to win the game, 39-38!

A Ravens defender grabs Giants quarterback Kerry Collins in Super Bowl XXXV. The Giants tried hard, but the Ravens were stronger.

Meet the Fans

Giants fans are like a big family. The team has been playing for many, many years. The fans have been cheering for that long, too! Grandparents, parents, and children all cheer together. Lots of fans have been sitting in the same seats for many years. Giants fans sometimes call their team the "Jints." That's a short way of saying "Giants."

Giants fans welcomed their team back home at New York City Hall after the team won the Super Bowl.

Heroes Then . . .

In the early days of the NFL, players played both offense and defense. They might never leave the field! Mel Hein played **center** on offense. He was a **linebacker** on defense. At both positions, he was one of the all-time best! In the 1950s, Emlen Tunnell starred at **defensive back**. His 79 **interceptions** are one of the highest totals ever. Y. A. Tittle was a star quarterback for the Giants. He led them to three NFL Championship Games. Frank Gifford was a speedy runner and **receiver**. In the 1980s, linebacker Lawrence Taylor became one of the best players ever . . . at any position. He was almost impossible to block. Tiki Barber stopped playing in 2007. He was a quick and clever **running back**.

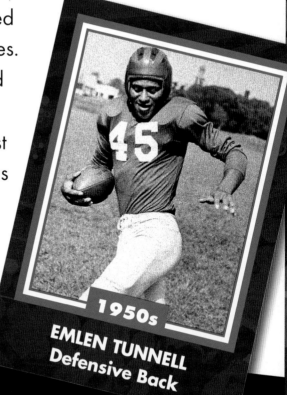

1950s
EMLEN TUNNELL
Defensive Back

Lawrence Taylor (left) used his awesome speed to go after opponents.

Heroes Now . . .

A quarterback named Manning led the Giants to a Super Bowl win in 2008. It was not the famous Peyton Manning. It was Peyton's younger brother, Eli! Eli has become one of the NFL's top passers. The Giants' running game is led by powerful running back Brandon Jacobs. On defense, New York depends on **defensive end** Justin Tuck. He's a great **pass rusher**.

ELI MANNING
Quarterback

BRANDON JACOBS
Running Back

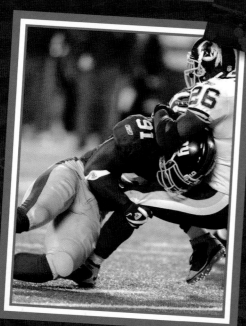

JUSTIN TUCK
Defensive End

25

Gearing Up

New York Giants players wear lots of gear to help keep them safe. They wear pads from head to toe. Check out this picture of Eli Manning and learn what NFL players wear.

The Football

NFL footballs are made of four pieces of leather. White laces help the quarterback grip and throw the ball. Inside the football is a rubber bag that holds air.

Football Fact

NFL footballs don't have white lines around them. Only college teams use footballs with those lines.

helmet

facemask

shoulder pad

chest pad

hand warmer

thigh pad

knee pad

cleats

27

Sports Stats

Note: All numbers are through the 2008 season.

Touchdowns

TOUCHDOWN MAKERS

These players have scored the most touchdowns for the Giants.

PLAYER	TOUCHDOWNS
Frank Gifford	78
Tiki Barber	68

PASSING FANCY

Top Giants quarterbacks

PLAYER	PASSING YARDS
Phil Simms	33,462
Charlie Conerly	19,488

Quarterbacks

RUN FOR GLORY

Top Giants running backs

PLAYER	RUSHING YARDS
Tiki Barber	10,449
Rodney Hampton	6,897

Running backs

Receivers

CATCH A STAR
Top Giants receivers

PLAYER	CATCHES
Amani Toomer	668
Tiki Barber	586

TOP DEFENDERS
Giants defensive records

Most interceptions: Emlen Tunnell, 74

Most **sacks**: Michael Strahan, 141.5

Defenders

COACH
Most Coaching Wins

Steve Owen, 153

Coach

Glossary

artificial fake, not real

center a player on the offensive line who snaps, or hikes, the ball to the quarterback

defense players who are trying to keep the other team from scoring

defensive back a defensive player whose main job is preventing receivers from making catches

defensive end a player who tries to tackle the other team's quarterback and running backs

end zone a 10-yard-deep area at each end of the field

hash marks short white lines that mark off each yard on the football field

interceptions catches made by defensive players

linebacker a defensive player who begins each play standing behind the main defensive line

line of scrimmage the place where the two teams face off when a play starts

offense players who have the ball and are trying to score

pass rusher a defensive player who tries to tackle the quarterback or stop him from passing

quarterback the key offensive player who starts each play and passes or hands off to a teammate

receiver an offensive player who catches forward passes

rivalry an ongoing competition between teams that play each other often, over a long time

running back an offensive player who runs with the football and catches passes

sacks tackles of a quarterback behind the line of scrimmage

Super Bowl the NFL's yearly championship game

touchdown a six-point score made by carrying or catching the ball in the end zone

Find Out More

BOOKS

Buckley, James Jr. *The Scholastic Ultimate Book of Football*. New York: Scholastic, 2009.

Doeden, Matt. *Eli Manning*. Minneapolis: Twenty-First Century Books, 2008.

Madden, John, and Bill Gutman. *Heroes of Football*. New York: Dutton, 2006.

Polzer, Tim. *Play Football! A Guide for Young Players from the National Football League*. New York: DK Publishing, 2002.

Stewart, Mark. *The New York Giants*. Chicago: Norwood House Press, 2006.

WEB SITE

Visit our Web site for lots of links about the New York Giants and other NFL football teams:

childsworld.com/links

Note to Parents, Teachers, and Librarians: We routinely verify our Web links to make sure they are safe, active sites—so encourage your readers to check them out!

Index

About the Author

K. C. Kelley is a huge football fan! He has written dozens of books on football and other sports for young readers. K. C. used to work for NFL Publishing and has covered several Super Bowls.